Mass Psychology 101

How To Control, Influence, Manipulate And Persuade A Group Of People Or Audience

By William Legend

I0455485

Table of Contents

INTRODUCTION

It's Friday night in a packed nightclub. The bass is pounding. The disco ball is twirling. This week, numerous terrorist acts have been broadcast from around the world, and everyone is weary of hearing about death and destruction. They're here to dance, drink, flirt, and have a good time.

Half of the partygoers are dancing in stilettos or tight pants, and the other half are consuming cocktails and beers at twice the normal rate because of peer pressure and the half off deal the club is offering tonight.

Sometime around 1 AM, one very drunk guy thinks it would be funny to shout, "Fire!" and see what happens. The only people who hear him over the pounding live music are his buddies, and they laugh. Then they all take turns shouting out natural disasters and then man-made disasters. It's like the penis game, but instead of shouting inane body parts, they're shouting politically charged phrases intended to scare people.

Eventually, someone nearby hears something about terrorists and asks his buddy what's going on. Before the theory can be crushed, it's circulating the club that the band playing for them is a front for a terrorist group, and everyone in the room is going crazy. Some people sneak out the door before anything terrible can happen. Some people are screaming. Others are throwing things at the band.

By the time management realizes there's a problem, things are wildly out of control, and no one knows what's actually going on. Even the guys who had been shouting random stuff are afraid, because some people are throwing punches at them to get to the door and get out of the club. What began as a bit of fun has turned into something scary.

Management calls the police, and the sirens add to the fear. The music is shut off. The disco ball is halted. The band is held in the break room. The hundreds of drunken partiers are kicked out. Even by the time the chaos has been eliminated, no one knows exactly what happened. What made the crowd go crazy? What were they suddenly afraid of? Can such a thing be prevented in the future?

What Is Mass Psychology?

People behave and react differently to things in groups than they do as individuals. A guy at a club with his buddies is almost always going to feel more confident and be more willing to try crazier things than the guy who came alone.

By herself, Annie might never get the urge to take eight shots in rapid succession and then go make out with strangers and dance on tabletops, but with her friends, she turns into a party animal willing to take just about any suggestion thrown out there.

As you are well aware, humans are social creatures, and we take a lot of our cues about what decisions to make from each other. Peer pressure doesn't end in grade school; once we've entered adulthood, our peers simply become more ambiguously defined.

Mass psychology, also called group or crowd psychology, is a facet of social psychology. As such, it is the study of the behaviors of groups of people. It's the study of how people behave when there are other people present, whether these are friends, colleagues, enemies, or random strangers. It's an attempt to discern and define how people behave when they are together.

This entire book is about exploring this phenomenon and showing you how you can harness these powers to meet your own goals.

As an individual, it's easy to assume that there's not a lot you can do to affect change within a large group, but such an assumption is misleading. Look at Martin Luther. Look at his namesake, Martin Luther King Jr. Look at Hitler. Whether for good or for bad, these individuals have succeeded at calling large groups of people to action in completely radical ways. Martin Luther began the first protestant church, breaking away from the church of the state. Martin Luther King Jr. persuaded many to fight for the civil rights cause in a nonviolent manner. Hitler persuaded his army to round up and brutally kill an entire race of people.

How was any of this possible? It didn't happen simply because the individual decided to put his all into achieving his goal. It didn't happen simply because he had a dream or an idea. It happened through the intricacies of group psychology. You can have all the willpower in the world and never succeed in persuading your high school class to vote you senior class president. You can believe in yourself one hundred percent of the way and still fall painfully short of your mark without an understanding of how groups function.

Group persuasion isn't as much about determination as it is about psychology. This book will clue you in on the psychology you will need to successfully take control in a group setting by explaining how human minds work together, by giving you examples of how this works, and by giving you practical suggestions you can use to persuade groups. The focus of this book is on practicality. As such, it won't read like a scientific treatise but as a friend imparting knowledge for your benefit.

Perhaps you will find much of the information in this book to be fairly intuitive. If that's the case, congratulations! You probably have a natural affinity for understanding people and how they behave in groups. If that's the case, this book will give you a vocabulary for your intuitive knowledge and hopefully give you some new ways to use your intuitive understanding to meet your goals.

Even if something as complex as the human mind is as mystifying to you as quantum mechanics, this book will break it down for you and leave you with a newfound understanding of what it means for you to persuade a group of people to behave in a certain way.

This book will give you detailed answers to questions like: How much power does an individual have over a group, and how do they obtain that power? Why and how do people conform? To what extent is behavior contagious? Do people always act in line with their beliefs? Do these beliefs change based on which group they are in?

The purpose of this book is to flesh out the answers to these questions and more in greater detail to show you how you can control, influence, manipulate, and persuade any group or audience.

CHAPTER ONE: CONFORMITY

Ben isn't the raving liberal his friends think he is. In fact, if anyone were to ask him one-on-one about his beliefs in terms of lifestyle, they would find that he lives a fairly conservative life. He recycles. He's faithful to his wife. He plays with his kids every evening when he gets home from work. He has set up college funds for each of his kids and makes regular payments to those funds. He has a beer on occasion but nothing too crazy. He shows up to work on time and does more or less his best on most days. He has good credit and doesn't max out his credit cards on things he can't afford. He gets his family to church for the main holidays. He takes his family on two big vacations every year.

But when he's out with his partying buddies from college, he downplays all of this, instead talking up that time he went partying with some guys from work and pissed his wife off (it was a bachelor party, and she was only a little mad that he forgot to tell her which night it was), or that time he got trashed at a barbeque and bet a bunch of money on the Vikings winning the Super Bowl (he was actually only buzzed, and it was twenty bucks).

When he's with these guys he used to have so much in common with, he reverts back to his immature college self and joins in on the banter as if nothing in his life has changed. A desperate urge to fit in overcomes him, and he says and does what he needs to in order to fit in with them. If they do shots, he does shots. If they flirt with women half their age, he laughs along with them. If they tell him to go touch that cop's gun, he probably would.

It's no wonder Ben's wife refuses to find a babysitter and come with him on these outings.

What is Ben's problem?

It would appear that Ben has a simple case of conformity.

What is Conformity?

Conformity is what happens when people adjust their actions or beliefs in order to more closely match those of the group. Much of conformity happens on a subconscious level. Perhaps Ben in the above example doesn't realize how much he changes his behavior to fit in with his buddies. As soon as he walks through the doors into the bar, he transforms from a good husband and father and upright member of society to the obnoxious, cussing, hippie he used to be in college.

People tend to mimic the behaviors of others even subconsciously. If someone smiles, you probably smile back. If a bunch of people are running to the window to see what's going on outside in the yard, there's a good chance you'll follow, even if you know there's nothing there. Understanding how conformity works will help you in just about every aspect of group persuasion.

People conform for a variety of reasons, but they can generally be broken into two overall facets: normative social influence or informational social influence.

Normative social influence is when people try to avoid rejection or obtain social approval. Society has certain normative rules for accepted behavior. Violating such rules can result in paying a certain price, such as an injured reputation or social ostracizing.

A celebrity might defy social norms by taking her clothes off in public and become infamous overnight. A suburban mom might admit that she occasionally spanks her children when they willfully disobey her rules and be cut out of her entire social group.

Informational social influence is a type of influence that derives from one's willingness to accept other peoples' opinions about society or reality. If a thousand people are running for the hotel exit claiming that there's a fire, anyone in their right mind would sum up the situation by following the thousand people leaving the hotel. Only an extremely vain person will be completely unwilling to set aside his own beliefs about reality in order to pay attention to what others are saying or doing.

If everyone in a group is behaving in a certain way, the most common instinct is to conform, and there's certainly some value to this. If all of your friends and family members tell you that your haircut is bad, what are the chances that they are all jealous and lying? After all, they can't all be wrong, can they?

How Does Conformity Work?

You've probably noticed that when one person yawns, it often starts a chain of yawning with whoever saw the yawn. This is because human brains are wired for empathy. Our brains contain what are called mirror neurons, which help us observe and interpret the actions and expressions of others by recreating those actions or expressions inside of our own brains. Sometimes the recreated expression will then translate to our own bodies, as is often the case with yawning.

The more empathetic a person is, the more likely they are to subconsciously mimic others' behaviors. If a friend looks sad, it's natural to let your face reflect the same sadness that theirs does. If a friend looks happy, you are more likely to look and feel happy as well. If Cecelia's body language indicates that she is sad, her empathetic friends might adjust their own body language to match Cecelia's in order to show understanding and solidarity.

Perhaps you've gotten really into a football game and then suddenly realized that you were thumping your feet on the floor as the running back ran for the touchdown, as if you were trying to help him run faster.

Mirror neurons don't mandate that a person will conform to a certain behavior, however. Attitudes also play an important role in conformity. Attitudes are values or beliefs that predispose us to certain responses.

If I love cheeseburgers, and my friends are trying to persuade me that I should go with them to get a cheeseburger, their excitement might get my mirror neurons firing until I'm pumped and getting in the car with them to gladly break my New Year's diet.

On the other hand, if I was a vegetarian who hated cheeseburgers, my brain would recognize my friends' excitement, but my own values would prevent me from conforming to the group expectation. Because they are my friends, I might politely decline instead of giving them a speech on the animals that were tortured and killed to produce that burger, which is a speech I relish giving to strangers, but I won't conform and eat the burger.

Behavior tends to be contagious in groups, but only insofar as the appropriate attitudes are present. You might persuade a group of immigrants to work double shifts in your factory for less than minimum wage because they don't know English well enough to understand what they are agreeing to, and they desperately want a job, but you will be hard pressed to persuade a group of educated Americans to do the same thing, because their attitudes about what is fair and what jobs they are able to obtain are going to be a lot different.

Likewise, you might successfully persuade a crowd of social activists at a rally to storm the White house to support their cause, because the attitude of reform is strong in the room, and people are ready to take action, even though many of the same individuals would have declined such an invitation if you had asked them individually to storm the White house.

Because of an intrinsic desire for some level of conformity, groups make for a powerful mechanism for things like social justice. An individual at home on her couch might get mad about a proposed legislation to limit her religious freedom. She might be silently angry about the subject for a few weeks and then forget about her anger when the next controversial legislation comes around. But let's say that she finds herself in a group of likeminded individuals who are planning a protest. She will be a lot more likely to take actions that support her beliefs when she's part of this group.

Many of us who were raised in individualistic societies are taught that conformity is a bad thing. Sometimes it is. World War II is a prime example of conformity gone wrong, with people turning in their neighbors, killing, and ignoring injustices out of fear.

Sometimes conformity is seen as the easy way out. A lot of people are willing to meet the status quo in order to maintain or grow their standard of living. They go to their corporate nine to five jobs. They believe what their friends believe. They don't rock the boat unless they have to. They ignore injustices that seemingly have nothing to do with them.

When many of us think of conformity, we think of groupthink, a term coined by researcher Irving Janis to describe the harmonious but ineffectual planning that went into invading Cuba with 1400 Cuban exiles in 1961. The president at the time, John F. Kennedy, had just been elected, and he and his advisors were unswervingly optimistic about the plan. Because of Kennedy's optimism about the plan, others suppressed their opposing opinions in order to keep harmony within the group. The mission backfired, leaving the president and his advisors scratching their heads.

Groupthink is common in situations that discourage opposing views and present only a limited array of evidence for a claim. People who fall prey to groupthink tend to be overconfident and overly self-justifying.

Perhaps your mother has asked you, "If everyone jumped off a bridge, would you do it?"

"No, of course not. That's stupid," you say. But what if everyone is enthusiastically supporting the bridge-jumping plan and optimistically talking about the euphoria of freefalling? What if no one mentions any of the potential dangers? Informational social influence might lead you to believe that since everyone is doing it, and no one is talking about the dangers, then the dangers don't exist. Given these circumstances, there's a good chance that you'll find yourself jumping off of the bridge along with everyone else, despite the likelihood of a broken neck.

On the other hand, group conformity can be a powerful force for good in the world. Many charity organizations exist for the purpose of bringing together people with similar attitudes to help the hungry or the homeless or to bring aid to refugees or storm victims in other parts of the world. A lot of individuals have beliefs that they don't know how to act on. Being a member of a group brings them a sense of power and purpose in their lives.

How You Can Use Conformity as an Individual

All of this talk about the power of groups can make it seem like individuals have very little control or influence, but nothing could be further from the truth. If you want to persuade, the ball is in your court.

Community is a bedrock of human experience, and conformity is one of the methods by which communities continue to function on a daily level. Many thriving churches continue to thrive because of a certain level of group conformity within the church community. Members make a commitment to hold certain values like weekly donations and a commitment to helping the poor and disabled, and, in exchange, the community gives support to the members when they need it and a sense of overall life purpose.

If one does not already exist, start a community or group to bring together people who hold the same beliefs you do. It can be a physical or a virtual group.

If you hold a majority opinion, your road may already be paved for you. If you hold a minority opinion, the best things you can do to sway the majority opinion are to hold consistently to your beliefs and to be persistent.

If you keep changing your mind about what you believe people will have a hard time taking your side, even if you are making some good points. In the 2004 election, presidential candidate, John Kerry, was accused of flip-flopping on the war in Iraq due to a series of contradictory statements that he made on the subject. This, in part, lost him the election.

Basically, it's okay to have a contradictory opinion about something, as long as you don't contradict yourself. According to a study on minority influence by Wood et. al., people aren't that likely to change their public opinions to fit with a deviant view, but that if they change their private opinions or open themselves to think about minority views, it's because the minority view expressed was especially consistent (1994).

Aspects of conformity trickle into many of the group persuasion techniques that will be discussed in the rest of this book, because humans are social creatures. Some of us are natural leaders, but almost all of us are natural followers in some way, shape, or form, and conformity is how social groups maintain themselves.

CHAPTER TWO: THE IN-GROUP BIAS

Dolores is extremely loyal to her small town. Born and raised there, she comes to all of the town-wide events, knows all of the history backward and forward, and always defends the mayor's decisions to outsiders who criticize him. Whenever outsiders come to town, she even goes so far as to welcome them while making sure they know that they are not part of the in-group by singling out her fellow townspeople. She makes a point of referencing inside jokes more frequently than she normally would if there were no outsiders present.

In fact, many of the town's residents feel the same way. After all, not many towns could claim that Abraham Lincoln had campaigned there back in 1859 like they could. Their town still had the original schoolhouse built in 1836 that their grandparents trekked three miles uphill both ways to get to. They also were the only town in the state with a coffee pot for a water tower.

Their town might have had more domestic abuse reported than any town in the county, but they chalked it up to fire-y Irish tempers and laughed it off. Besides, the next town over had a much bigger arson and drug problem than they did, and at least they didn't have any gangs.

The mayor might be having factory waste dumped in the river, but no one had been able to prove that he was behind it. Besides, that factory employed most of the townspeople, so they needed it and were obligated to love it, even though it hadn't been in the original town blueprints. In Dolores's eyes, the factory was more of a source of life than the river, since it was what fed most of the town's families and paid their mortgages.

Whenever people, especially transplants to the town, try to speak out against the dangerous fourth of July tradition of firing guns into the sky in the field across from the city hall, Dolores is the first to remind the city council that the rich tradition of the town is what binds them all together and makes them a special community. The loyal townspeople always cheer at this, accentuating the fact that the person who moved to destroy the tradition is not part of the town's in-group.

Dolores's in-group bias has kept her from seeing and addressing some of the problems within her town even while it has contributed to the residents' feelings of belonging and camaraderie.

How Does In-group Bias Work?

Think back to your high school days. If you're in high school, think back to now. There was the in-crowd, the out-crowd, and the middle-dwelling-crowds, but no matter which crowd you were in, you probably experienced at least a small bit of in-group bias when it came to the other groups, clubs, or teams you identified yourself with.

A bias is a preference that is based in identity. You might identify yourself based on your religion, country, political party, sports team, knitting group, cat sitters' club, or any number of other groups, which by default exclude people who are not members of the group.

In-group bias is the tendency to favor one's own group and group members. If you have ever been on a sports team, you probably believed that your team was the best. If you were in a band, you believed that your band was the best. Even if you weren't quantitatively the best, you found other areas of excellence within your group, and you pointed them out to your group's members to foster your in-group bias and create a sense of group belonging and unity.

Any group that is not the in-group is the out-group. If you're on a swim team, the out-groups could be the other sports teams at your school or they could be the swim teams at other schools.

Studies show that most groups tend to reserve their strongest feelings of dislike for rival out-groups that are the most like them. For example, Protestant and Catholic Christians who are seen as having more commonalities than differences are often more competitive with each other than they are with other religions in some parts of the world. While a team of soccer players and a team of gymnasts might show some contempt for the other's sport or feel competitive about who is more athletic, the two teams will probably reserve their most intense competitive feelings for the soccer teams of gymnasts against whom they will actually compete.

There is also a tendency among groups to see all out-group or non-group people as being the same as each other. Dolores from the above example sees the people in her town as being superior, and everyone who is not in her town is equally inferior, whether they come from the next town over or from across the world.

In-groups function on an "us versus them" mentality. Group members separate themselves from the out-groups with justifications for why they are better. Sometimes in-groups are as trivial as a sports team affiliation, and sometimes they are as severe as a race or class identity.

The rich may identify the most with other rich people and reinforce among their in-group the belief that they deserve their wealth and should act in ways that protect their standing within this in-group. Certain races may identify their racial group as "better" and thus reinforce racial stereotypes and deepen the divides between races.

How You Can Use In-group Bias to Influence

In-group biases will always exist, so, as a persuader, you might as well learn how to take advantage of these built-in affections and loyalties and use them to form persuasive arguments or implement new ideas.

If you need certain people to accept you or agree with you, come up with ways to show that you are, in fact, part of their group. If you want to run for president as part of the Republican Party, you need to show the party members that you believe in the same things they do and that you want to push their agendas as much as they do. Or show that you have a deep wallet and an obnoxious head of hair that will translate well into the political cartoons in the Sunday paper.

Maybe you want to establish yourself as a member of an elite moms club at your son's private school, so you join the PTA, wear the same posh clothing brands as the other moms, and make a point of your gluten-free diet, which they all share. If you look and act like them, a lot of times people tend to assume that you are part of their group and give you the preferential treatment that the in-group members receive.

You might have a painful bone disease, but if you find a way to look and act healthy, people will assume that you are healthy and treat you as they would a healthy person by becoming infuriated when you pull into a handicapped parking spot.

A technique you can use to foster group unity is called group polarization. Group polarization is what happens when a group discusses its views in such a way that it enhances the primary views within the group. By encouraging your group to talk about its strengths, you also encourage the unity within the group and increase the likelihood of unanimous group decisions that seem to benefit your group.

Group polarization takes place in childhood between boys and girls. It is the phenomenon whereby boys become more like other boys by spending most of their time with boys, and girls become more like other girls by spending most of their time with girls. As boys and girls grow up in their separate gender-based groups, the differences become more pronounced, with girls preferring home-based games like house and dolls and boys preferring more physically-based games like wrestling and sports.

Of course, these social stereotypes are not true for all boys and girls. In fact, it can be argued that boys and girls tend to assign themselves these differences as an artificial means of identifying themselves more strongly as male or female based on what adults have modeled for them.

Political activists for political parties become more deeply enmeshed in their own politics by talking with others who believe the same things. After talking with his liberal coworkers about the death penalty, Eric feels more strongly than ever that the death penalty should be gotten rid of.

People tend to gravitate toward people who share and affirm their opinions and avoid those who disagree with them. Repeated affirmation of beliefs not only makes a person or group more complacent, or polarized, in their own beliefs, but it also makes them more likely to think of someone with different or opposing beliefs as the "other" or the out-group.

The CEO of a company might be trying to persuade the shareholders not to sell out their shares to another company even though the market is down by encouraging them to talk about how their money and input have been invaluable to the company's growth and influence over the last decade. If this goes as planned, the investors will start to feel a sense of pride at belonging to such an elite group and decide not to sell out the company to this other company, which is not nearly as good as theirs.

Group polarization is good to keep in mind for a variety of reasons. The first is when you are thinking about creating your own group for a certain purpose, and you are deciding which people you want to include. People are more likely to make a riskier decision when they are in a group versus deciding individually, which makes group polarization particularly handy when you need to get everyone on board with a risky plan.

If you want a group that will make risky decisions, choose people who are most likely to make more drastic choices in groups and under pressure. On the other hand, if you need people who will stay calm and maintain the status quo, choose more conservative people to be members of your group.

Basically, choose the people who will get done what you need them to get done. If you want to start a committee to beautify the city, don't choose people who are fine with how the city is presently; choose people who are eager for change. This sounds obvious, but it's not always as easy as it sounds, especially when you also need to find funding for your project. Sometimes the people with the money to fund a certain project and the people most likely to get caught up in an upward spiral of risky decision-making don't line up. In this case you will need to make sure that there are enough risk-takers in the group to pass your agenda, even if a few of the members are more cautious.

A technique you might need to use to convince a group that they should stick with you when things go awry is referred to as the scapegoat theory. The scapegoat theory, as you are probably aware, is a method of redirecting blame in order to keep a group from rising up in opposition against you or another member of the group.

For example, a boss who is laying off a bunch of employees after a series of corporate-mandated budget cuts might send his assistant to give out the notices to the employees so that he doesn't have to personally deal with the fallout of the situation. In the same way, the assistant might blame the boss for choosing who to keep and who to let go. In their own way, both the boss and the assistant have chosen a scapegoat to redirect the blame to someone else.

If you persuaded the group to purchase an expensive new coffeemaker with a no refund policy, and it broke the week after you got it, people might blame you for persuading them to buy such a piece of junk in the first place. Group members might choose sides, and dissention will replace harmony. However, if you can calmly explain that the company that made the coffee machine falsely advertised their product and that it was unfair of them to send you a broken product, it might encourage your group members to redirect their anger at the coffee machine company and diffuse any group dissention.

How To Infiltrate an In-group

Sometimes, you won't be the appointed leader in a particular group. You might even be an outsider. When this is the case, there are a few nifty tricks to keep in mind when you are trying to infiltrate an in-group or redirect its attention to more important things.

It's worth noting that group lines are not always straightforward, and many groups overlap in such a way that rivalries can both exist and be put on hold for the greater good of the larger group.

Families are a great example of this. Siblings might fight and compete with each other unmercifully, but if someone outside of the family starts a fight with one of their own, the family members will become allies against a common foe. Even the Capulets and Montagues will align themselves temporarily if the Romans attack Verona. In this case, the good of the larger group, the city, trumps the vicious interfamily battle.

Another method you can use to get your way in an in-group is to suggest that doing what you say will set them even further apart from the perceived out-groups. If you want taxpayers to vote to build a new multi-million dollar school in the district, you might point out that the proposed design is more elegant and more technologically advanced than the school buildings in any of the other districts in the area. Voting to build the school will thus make your district even more superior to the others.

CHAPTER THREE:
DEINDIVIDUATION

College basketball fans dress up in the team colors to cheer on their team at the big nationals game. They put on face paint, carry giant flags, and bring obnoxious noisemakers with them. Feeling anonymous and excited by the game and the surroundings, fans yell out at the referees when calls are made against their team, and they scream with excitement whenever their players make a basket.

As the game heats up, trash talk against the opposing team and its fans becomes more caustic and distracting for the players. The fans aggressively boo the players on the opposing team when they score. They also boo the referee who dares to call a foul on their player.

When their team loses, the incensed fans act as a group with one mind, pouncing and beating up the other team's pumped fans and yelling in the referees' faces for making bad calls and causing them to lose the game.

Campus security is summoned, and the worst offenders are brought in for questioning. No longer in the heat of the moment and lacking the anonymity of the large group, the violent individuals are confused and apologetic at their own behavior. They don't know what came over them; they insist that they wouldn't normally act that way.

The school officials look into their student records and see that most of the records are spotless. These seem to be good kids who merely got caught up in the haze of the group's fury.

These violent sports fans have fallen prey to deindividuation.

What is Deindividuation?

To some extent, people always lose a bit of their own identity when they are joined by other people in an activity. The more people there are, the more personal identity evaporates and melds to the group identity. Unless you are a very egotistical person with a low tolerance for informational social influence, you will experience this temporary fading of personal identity when you are part of a group.

Deindividuation is the word used to describe this loss of self-awareness and restraint that can sometimes happen in group situations. Three things make group deindividuation possible: arousal, a feeling of anonymity, and a large group.

Arousal can include anger, excitement or any extreme emotional state from which extreme actions may arise. This could be a protest, a sports game, a traffic jam, a musical performance, or any number of potentially emotional scenarios.

A feeling of anonymity comes from being only a single member of a large group. As one in a million, so to speak, the feeling of personal responsibility is diffused by the size of the group. Since the blame for an action is shared with the group, the individuals feel less personally responsible. The anonymous and irresponsible feeling is often accentuated through the use of face paint, uniforms, masks, costumes, sunglasses, and other items that might serve to hide or disguise personal identity.

Group members who depersonalize themselves in this manner are more likely to behave in more extreme ways in accordance with what the group is doing. They are no longer acting as identifiable individuals, but a facet of the whole group.

The size of the group matters in the extent of the deindividuation. The bigger the group, the more anonymous people feel, and the more diffused their responsibility for their actions feels. Deindividuation can still occur in a smaller group, but it's generally not going to happen on the same level. A high school wrestling team might wreck a hotel room, but a thousand angry protesters in face paint might burn down a factory that refuses to cut back its dangerous emissions.

Unlike basic conformity, deindividuation isn't necessarily about fitting in with group norms, acceptance, or any assumption that the group knows best. It usually occurs subconsciously or accidentally, and individuals often later have a difficult time explaining their behavior in rational terms.

Many people who wouldn't ordinarily go streaking on a dare might consider doing so if they are with a hundred other streakers who are all wearing masks.

Deindividuation can be a great way to get people to do morally questionable or even reprehensible acts without feeling like they need to take on so much of the personal blame for them. The KKK members wore hooded costumes and went out in groups to find and lynch African Americans. Their disguise gave them the confidence they needed to perform morally reprehensible acts against other fellow humans.

In wartime, armies will wear uniforms to battle in order to conceal identity and deindividuate. They will also work to dehumanize the enemy to make it easier to kill.

A person up on a bridge contemplating suicide after a rough breakup might be holding up traffic. Several of the backed-up commuters are annoyed and start honking and yelling at her to jump already so they can get home for supper. More motorists join in until the woman finally jumps to her death. Most people would be appalled that anyone would respond that way to a person who is experiencing such a tragic moment. Yet in the heat of the moment and fueled by a feeling of anonymity and lack of personal responsibility, people can be predictably evil.

Studies have even supported this phenomenon. A group of researchers observed children trick-or-treating on Halloween one year to see how they would react when they were told they could have one piece of candy and then were left alone or with a group of other children on the stoop to decide if they should take one piece of candy or cheat and take more.

After a researcher answered the door, she asked some of the children for their names before telling them to take a piece of candy. Some of the children came to the door alone, and some were in groups. She asked some lone children and some groups of children for their names, and some she did not. After telling all of them that they could each have one piece of candy, she retreated into the house, leaving them with a full bowl of candy.

When the children were observed through a secret peephole, it was noted that the children who came alone and gave their names took only one piece of candy nine out of ten times, whereas in the groups of anonymous children sixty percent stole candy, and many of them stole as much candy as they could (Deiner et. al., 1976) (McRaney, 2011).

The more anonymous or masked the children felt, the less inhibited they felt when it came to deliberately disobeying the rules that were clearly laid out for them.

How To Deindividuate

As you now know, three factors are typically at play in a deindividuated group: arousal, anonymity, and numbers.

So far this chapter has included destructive examples of deindividuation, but the technique can be used in a positive manner as well.

When deindividuation occurs at an individual level, a person immerses herself in an enjoyable activity like reading or painting, or playing a sport. Many scientists and experts have called this feeling of immersion and self-forgetfulness flow, hyperfocus, being in the zone, meditation, open-focus, the Silva Method, and any number of other names. This temporary loss of personal identity is achieved through distractions from one's own mindfulness. On a group level, the "distractions" previously mentioned were the war paint and emotionally charged setting.

If you want to motivate your group members to act in a way they normally wouldn't, you can dress them in war paint put them in an emotionally extreme situation, throw the first punch yourself, and then watch them finish the task.

But let's say that instead of performing acts of violence, you want to get a group to help a local farmer paint his barn. You might get the group members matching tee shirts and then fire them up about making the world a better place through community service. The individuals might then be able to lose themselves in the excitement of serving in a fun group and temporarily forget about any personal discomfort associated with the task of painting a barn.

Many church groups feel inspired to spread the love of Jesus through community service work and find that the service work is immersive. They forget about their own identities for the sake of the group identity. They want others to see their group as loving and caring, and this desire to meet their group goals trumps their own personal desires.

A lot of people get stage fright at the thought of singing solos for an audience, but yet they would happily sing in a choir. They are doing the same activity—singing in public—but the presence of a larger group spreads out the responsibility if something were to go wrong. One member of the choir can forget to come in at the right time, and the mistake is masked by the singing of the other members.

This is useful to keep in mind, because if you want to persuade an individual to do something that seems to daunting or scary, offering to get a bunch of other people to do it with them might diffuse the fear and the sense of individual responsibility they would be required to take in the event that something goes wrong.

If you want your marketing team to go door to door and ask homeowners a series of questions, not many of them will jump at that opportunity, but if you tell them they can bring a partner or go in small groups, they might balk a little less at the assignment.

How To Diffuse Deindividuated Groups

If you find yourself in the precarious position of needing to persuade a deindividuated group to calm itself or stop being violent, here are a few techniques you can use to diffuse the situation.

Your goal is to bring the group members back to their sense of self, so, if at all possible, use their names. As with the trick-or-treating children, people who remember who they are will be less likely to make destructive decisions. Where they have depersonalized the situation for themselves, personalize it. If applicable, remind them of what their families, friends, or significant others would think of their behavior.

Another way to bring back self-awareness is to simply inform the group members of what they are doing. Get up on a soapbox with a megaphone and start giving them the play-by-play if you have to.

Had you been at the basketball game disaster at the beginning of this chapter, you might have said something like: "You all came out for the game to have a good time and cheer on our team, but now you're beating up referees and shoving around the other team's fans. You've made parents bleed and children cry. You have shamed your school and your city."

On a slightly different note, in order to break the opposing football team's focused concentration while the game is in session, you might single out a player and ask him a personal question. Bringing him back to his own identity instead of the group identity might cause him to slip up or fumble the ball.

CHAPTER FOUR: SOCIAL FACILITATION

Geraldine is a ballerina at the National Ballet Academy. She has worked hard for most of her life perfecting her dance technique and artistry such that all of the movements come as naturally to her as breathing. She can perform a wide range of solos without having to consciously think through or review the steps before executing them. Now that her formal ballet education is almost done, she's auditioning for some very competitive spots in different ballet companies and troupes.

She's a beautiful dancer even when she's relaxed and practicing by herself in front of the mirror in her studio, but with the adrenaline pumping through her body resulting from the anticipation of a performance in front of judges, her senses are heightened, and she's able to bring her solo to a whole new level in her audition.

Her *grand jété* is elegant and smooth in rehearsal, but during her audition, it is higher and more effortless than she's ever done it. Her body knows the motions so well that her concentration is on the crook of her little finger, the slight tilt of her head during a *demi plié*, and her invisible intake of breath as she executes a series of complicated spins in rapid succession.

Whether she makes it into the troupe or not, she knows that she has given a stellar performance that has set the bar high for the other dancers who are auditioning for the same spot.

Geraldine has experienced something called of social facilitation.

What Is Social Facilitation?

Social facilitation is when a person performs more strongly on simple or well-learned tasks in the presence of other people or an audience of some kind than they do alone. In the above example, Geraldine's performance of a well-learned solo was enhanced when she performed it in front of the judges.

An athlete or a musician might perform better in front of an audience than he does in practice. This explains why a choir that sounds mediocre during the dress rehearsal might come on stage and knock it out of the park during the performance.

A good musician won't practice his scales until he gets them right; he will practice them until he can't get them wrong. That way, when he shows up for his audition, he's prepared to wow the judges. He might find that he can play them perfectly and more quickly than he did when he was practicing.

A lot of people experience a rush that pushes them to do better than normal when they perform for a crowd. Maybe you can't drink a full gallon of milk in under ten minutes at home by yourself, but when you're with the guys, you chug that thing and willingly suffer the consequences while you receive your well-deserved back slaps and fist bumps afterward.

This goes both ways, however. If a task is simple or complex but mastered, a group might perform better in the presence of an audience or competitor, but if the task is complicated and is not mastered, then the group is more likely to mess up or not do as well in front of others than it did during practice.

If you've ever had an oral exam in front of your classmates, you probably understand this phenomenon. If you've studied well enough, you might do better on the exam than you anticipated based on your practice tests and study guides. If you didn't study adequately, you are likely to look less prepared than you actually are.

A speechmaker will do better in front of the audience than he will do in front of his mirror if he has practiced sufficiently. On the other hand, if he's ill-prepared, the presence of the audience might cause him to stumble over his speech, stutter, forget portions, or go over or under the time limit.

Perhaps while learning to juggle, you finally start to get the hang of it and can do it by yourself in front of a mirror, but when you try to show someone, you keep dropping the bowling pins and look like you have two left hands.

Much of your individual experience with social facilitation can be extrapolated to groups as well. A group that is prepared will often exceed its own expectations when others are present. A group that is unprepared is likely to fail spectacularly with the presence of an audience.

A well-trained army can sometimes overcome seemingly insurmountable odds in face of battle, especially when there's a lot at stake. We see this happen repeatedly throughout history. The Carthaginian General Hannibal repeatedly beat down the Roman army, which outnumbered his own ragtag group by three and four times the men, making it all the way to the gate of the city of Rome before he was forced to turn back.

How To Use Social Facilitation In Group Persuasion

The Yerkes-Dodson Law will help explain how you can use social facilitation to persuade and motivate people to improve their performance. The Yerkes-Dodson Law states that there is a quantifiable relationship that occurs between performance and arousal. You've probably heard that some stress is good and too much stress is bad.

The Yerkes-Dodson law also implies that too little stress is also bad. Stress spurs motivation, and without enough of it, a person doesn't feel sufficiently motivated to perform well.

Let's say you want to increase the performance of your company's employees. You might use the social facilitation concept to do so in few different ways. You might try installing cameras in obvious places and letting the employees know that their work is being monitored at all times.

Since they perceive that they have a constant audience, they might be more likely to work faster or harder or take fewer bathroom breaks outside of the designated break times than they did before.

Cameras might work in some places of employment for a short time, but in others, they might simply lead people to feel spied on and thus have an opposite effect than what you intended. Eventually, when the cameras fade into the fabric of the workplace, employees will become less stressed about their presence and thus no longer feel sufficiently motivated to exceed their quotas or goals during the day.

You might instead create a more competitive atmosphere within the workplace pitting teams against each other to see who can create the greatest output. This might work especially well if you have multiple assembly lines and have daily quotas that need to be met. This is likely to work most effectively if the teams you create look and feel like they are competing against each other. Instead of pitting one floor of the building against the other, you might pit lines on the same floor against each other and keep a scoreboard that all of the employees can easily see.

For social facilitation to work effectively in your manmade competitive atmosphere, all of your employees must be properly trained. If someone hasn't received enough training and is still unsure about some of the procedures, the competitive atmosphere will have an opposite effect, slowing production down instead of speeding it up. This lack of training combined with the competition will drive the stress level too high for productivity and undermine your otherwise good strategy.

Be careful not to make the competition too fierce. If you hang a lot on the line for your employees or require nearly impossible results, the stress level might also become inhibiting, even for well-trained employees. Now instead of having a healthy level of stress from a friendly competition, your employees are facing debilitating test anxiety.

Your goal is to create just the right amount of productive stress to more efficiently accomplish the tasks at hand. The more menial the task is, the more stress you can add. On the other hand, the more complex the task is, the smaller your margin of error is in terms of stress. With too little stimulation, your employees won't have the motivation or energy to get their minds into the task. With even a little too much stress, they are overwhelmed and debilitated and unable to perform at optimum levels.

Maybe you need to motivate a team of volunteers to do a lot of fundraising for a charity organization, so you set up a friendly rivalry between your team and another team of volunteers that works for your organization. The social element of the activity might motivate the two groups to surpass their goals simply because the other group is watching their progress. Both groups' productivity levels are likely to increase just from the added presence of the other group.

The simpler a task is, the more arousal, or stress, a person or group will be able to handle to efficiently complete the task. For example, a sprinter's task is fairly simple. He wants to run as fast as he can for the designated short distance. Pretty much the more pumped up he is, the faster he will sprint.

To translate that for a group, let's say you've created an assembly line wherein each person has one simple, repetitive task. You might blast music to increase the energy in the room and spur the assembly line workers to move faster.

The more complex the task is, the more careful you have to be with distractions and levels of arousal. A person can't perform a complex task while half asleep, but too much stress, like an excess of anger or frustration, will be inhibiting. If you need a group to create a presentation for your next conference, you need them to be awake and excited enough to come up with an intelligent, attractive presentation, but you don't want them to be so overwhelmed by the task that they shut down and miss the boat on the goals of the presentation.

Don't forget that stress doesn't always have to mean mental stress caused by emotions. Sometimes, a stressor can simply be something that is a distraction from the assignment. The radio playing at a moderate background level might encourage energy and wakefulness while a group of architects draws up a blueprint for the new hospital, but a blasting radio might give them a sensory overload and slow the flow of their ideas.

If you are the leader of a group of some kind, it is your job to monitor the stress levels of your group members, because these levels of stress in relation to a certain task will determine the possible range of your group's productivity.

Just as you can seek to motivate groups through social facilitation, you can also motivate yourself by putting yourself in group situations that increase your own performances and overall persuasiveness.

If you've ever trained for a marathon and then run in the competition, you understand how drastically different the competition is from the training. It's the same repetitive motions and the same distances, but the entire experience feels different. The training felt like drudgery. You'd run the same laps or the same stretch of road feeling the soreness in your muscles every step of the way and trying to entertain yourself for one more mile and then another.

During the competition you are surrounded by other competitors and cheering sections along the way. When you see others near you in the street who are still running, you feel motivated to keep going. You're doing the same activity, but with people surrounding you who all have the same goal, you are able to maintain a higher energy level for a longer period of time.

Even better than running by yourself is group running. Having others with you who have the same goals will help you keep going longer than you believed you could and vice versa. You've probably heard the phrase "three strands of cord are not easily broken." What that means is that people are typically stronger in groups than they are as individuals. Groups make it harder for an individual to give up without losing face among the group members.

As a leader, it's easy enough to give a series of instructions and arrange friendly competitions, but sometimes the most motivating thing you can do for your team is to work alongside them. Let them know that their goals are your goals and that you are also working to achieve them. Naturally, this won't be practical in every situation, but whenever it is, your presence may be more of a social facilitation than any new rules or hidden cameras installed on the workroom floor.

Social facilitation works both ways: your presence might motivate your group to be better and faster, and their presence might motivate you to be better and faster.

CHAPTER FIVE: SOCIAL LOAFING

During election season, thousands of Americans participate in campaigning for certain candidates. They go door to door, hand out fliers, put up signs, speak at rallies, and write longwinded arguments to submit to the opinion section of the local newspaper or post on social media. These groups of campaigners are very involved and are deeply invested in the results of the election. For the duration of the election season, many of them live and breathe politics.

Then there are the people who actively participate in the elections themselves, following all of the latest news on each candidate so that they can make an informed decision when it's time to vote. They don't go out campaigning, but they make sure they know what they think if anyone asks for their opinion, and they always show up to cast their ballot. A majority of Americans would like to believe that they fall into this category. They have informed thoughts and opinions, but their lives are not consumed by politics.

The third level is the social loafers. These are often the people who don't really follow elections, and they don't show up to vote either because they figure their vote doesn't really mean anything anyway, or they know everyone in their family is voting for their chosen candidate already, so it's already covered.

These people may or may not have strong, all-consuming opinions on politics, but their opinions don't necessarily derive from a few hours of careful, focused research. Many of them will see a post a friend made on social media and make a snap decision about it just to have an opinion to voice. Many more social loafers will avoid anything political altogether, refusing to take part in conversations that might turn political, because they don't like to be uncomfortable or cause a stir. They claim that they don't care or that political issues aren't important.

The presidential election makes such a great example of social loafing because the group (United States citizens who are eighteen or older) is so large that it's easy for millions of people to slip through the cracks and count on the other millions in the group to pick up the slack.

In the 2012 election, the voter turnout was 57.5 percent, with 93 million eligible voters not showing up to vote. For a country that's so vocal about its freedoms and so quick to fly into a tailspin at the thought of any rights or privileges being taken away, a large portion of eligible voters doesn't seem to think it's important enough to fill out a ballot in accordance with the rights and privileges they value most.

What Is Social Loafing?

Social loafing is the tendency for people in a group to make less of an effort when they are pooling their efforts to reach a common goal than when they are individually accountable for their effort or work. In the election example above, a small percentage of Americans make the most effort to get the word out there, and a little over half of them put in at least the minimal effort to vote. In any given election year as many as forty to fifty percent of eligible citizens don't vote at all.

People learn how social loafing works from a very young age. Think back to your grade school days when the teacher put you into groups to do projects. The smart kids in the class would often hate group work, because the other group members thought of group work as an opportunity to slack off and leave more of the work to the smart kid in the group.

Due to the knowledge of social loafing, some teachers would assign both group and individual grades for a project in order to minimize social loafing in groups, but even if all members worked equally as hard on their assigned project, chances were still good that they were individually putting in less of an effort than they would have put into a non-group assignment.

For example, maybe an individual will give their all to studying for the SATs, but when they're put into a group of people to work out a bunch of math problems, they might put only 80 percent of their effort into the task. They feel that since there are more people with whom to share the work, they are more anonymous and less personally accountable for the results that the group comes up with.

In a study by Ingham et. al. people were observed, and their effort was measured in a tug of war match. The study found that when coworkers were added one by one to a tug of war team, individual effort significantly declined which each coworker added (1974). Many other similar experiments have been conducted since then with similar conclusions.

Why do people tend to slack off in groups? It can come from the feeling of being dispensable. If they feel like their contribution could have been given just as well by anyone else, they might feel that they are unimportant to the group, and it's therefore not worth putting in a huge effort. Additionally, when group members know that they will receive equal parts of the reward no matter how much they contribute, they might feel like it doesn't matter if they slack.

In some communist societies, social loafing is a real trial for this very reason. Because everything done is for the good of the entire community, and there is no individual success without group success, individuals often feel comfortable with working less hard than they would have otherwise, since they are already entitled to a set share in the profits anyway.

Positive Effects of Social Loafing

In many group efforts, social loafing is seen as a negative, undesirable thing. In the instance of voting in the public elections, if the social loafers had gone to the polls and voted, many elections might have had drastically different results.

However, a good leader will see that there is some valuable insight that can be taken from the premises of social loafing. As a persuader, you should keep these in mind.

For example, Jericho is the supervisor for a design company, and a client has just come to him with a huge new project to design a set of brochures to advertise a line of health products. Jericho knows that he can assign the project to one of his team members to do the whole project, but all of them already have projects that they're working on individually and can't devote all of their time to pleasing this new client.

Instead of re-juggling the workloads to free up a designer, Jericho assigns the project to a group of three designers, telling them when the deadline is and that they must get together and decide how to conceptualize the project and divide the work up. Now instead of having one mind putting one hundred percent into the project, he has three minds putting eighty percent of their effort into it.

Because working in a group has broken down the stress level of the huge project between three different people, the designers are able to continue with their usual workload with minimal added stress. This keeps Jericho from having to put all the stress on a single designer.

The premises of social loafing, in this example, allowed for more work to get done in the same amount of time with minimal inhibiting stress, even though none of the group members could put their all into the project. Naturally, this kind of thing won't work in all types of groups, but in particularly motivated groups, it can do wonders.

Another example of when the premises of social loafing can offer some positive insight is in the event of an emergency of some kind. If one group member is incapable of picking up as much slack as the others, having a group will help spread out that extra stress.

When Mom is sick in bed, Dad does the cooking and laundry, and the kids help out with the dishes and pets to pick up the slack until Mom is better. In close-nit groups, such as family units, social loafing, whether purposeful or accidental, is a given, but the groups can find a way to take turns with days off so that the group doesn't fall behind in its task.

Intentionally dispersing segments of social loafing equally among group members throughout a schedule can, in some circumstances, make the group members more productive for having had the time off. The intentional loafing functions kind of like paid time off. This kind of schedule will work best if the project must be drawn out over a long period of time, whereas with a short project it will probably just create unnecessary confusion and delays.

How To Control Social Loafing

Before you form a group to get an assignment done, there are a few things you should keep in mind in order to minimize the bad kind of social loafing.

First of all, if the project is large, come up with a way to break it into segments. A long, large project is the easiest kind of project for people to get away with social loafing. If your project is huge and spread out over several months or years, it makes it harder to keep track of who has made what contributions to the group, and members feel like they can get away with doing less.

For example, a semester long group project in which students are creating a government for their own fictional country might be easy to put off until the last week of the semester, or the less motivated students might let the students who are most interested in the project do most of the work.

To keep social loafing in check, consider installing deadlines throughout the duration of the project or assigning each group member specific tasks that they must accomplish on their own in order to receive any credit.

Another factor that makes it easy for social loafers is a large group setting. The bigger the group is, the easier it is for individuals to get away with doing nothing or as little as possible. As you saw in the election example at the beginning of this chapter, when over a hundred million people are already voting, ninety-three million feel like they can get away with not doing anything.

Smaller groups provide less anonymity and greater feelings of individual responsibility. If you're worried about your group's social loafing, cut some members or divide the group into two or three groups so that more people feel like their input matters.

Thirdly, you can create a peer evaluation system throughout the course of the project. When group members know that their peers are evaluating their performance, they will be more likely to step up and contribute. No one likes being called out as a slacker. The potential of having to take personal responsibility for laziness can be a great motivator for some. You might also let the group know in advance that they will each be giving a report of what they personally contributed to the group output at the end of the project. After all, an opportunity to impress the boss with brilliant contributions to recount at the end might be far more motivating than making brilliant contributions that go unnoticed or only noticed at the group level.

Finally, the most effective way to oust social loafing from your group setting and influence higher group productivity is to make the group members feel more invested in the group itself. Members who are excited about being in the group and feel a strong sense of identity within the group will almost always produce more effective results than groups with low personal involvement.

The in-group bias and group polarization are concepts talked about earlier in this book that can help you out with minimizing social loafing by persuading your group members that they are part of something awesome and bigger than themselves.

Maybe a group of social workers is starting to get burned out by the constant onslaught of paperwork and bureaucratic hoops they have to jump through to help out families and children, and they're starting to slack off and leave more work to their newer and still optimistic coworkers. Reminding them of their greater purpose and of how much good they've done for individual families might help them step outside of the tedium of every day and see their identity within a bigger picture.

CHAPTER SIX: FOOT-IN-THE-DOOR

Volunteers for a local charity organization were going door to door to raise funds for a rape awareness campaign. The volunteers asked homeowners in their neighborhood to give a donation, saying that even a dollar would help support their cause more than they knew. Many of the residents ended up giving at least a dollar.

A couple of weeks later, the volunteers came around again, this time asking for ten dollars to support their cause. Those who had previously given a dollar or more the last time around were the most likely to give the ten dollar donation compared with those who had refused to donate anything.

The volunteers were taking advantage of the foot-in-the-door phenomenon.

What Is Foot-In-The-Door Phenomenon?

Foot-in-the-door phenomenon is what happens when people who first agreed to a small request later gave in to a larger request. Actions feed attitudes and attitudes feed actions. When a person agrees to give a small donation at first, they are more likely to later give a larger donation to the same organization the next time around. When you cave and finally buy yourself a box of Girl Scout cookies this year, you are more likely cave and buy yourself two or three boxes next year.

Maybe you ask a group of people to donate just a dollar to your cause. Next year rolls around, and you ask the same people to just donate two dollars. They remember that they donated to your organization last year, and they are more willing to do so again. Their past self gives them the confidence to repeat the action of donating this year, and you've succeeded at bringing in twice the donations as last year.

Foot-in-the-door phenomenon is effective at paving the way toward getting people to do things that they find to be personally objectionable or even morally questionable. A child might throw a tantrum in the supermarket in order to get a piece of candy. The parents give in, and the child now has a foot in the door. The parents have already agreed to the candy. The child intuitively knows that now that they've given in to the tantrum once, they're now more likely to next time agree to the cake and then the small toy and then the more expensive toy.

Foot-in-the-door phenomenon can feel a lot like a slippery slope.

A boyfriend might persuade his girlfriend to take off her shirt for him. Next time he sees her, he asks her to remove more of her clothing. Because she already agreed to the first request, she's more likely to agree to the second request, even if she doesn't really want to or doing so goes against her boundaries or moral code.

People want their attitudes and their actions to line up. When they give in to something small that they don't necessarily agree with, they are opening themselves to the possibility that they might subconsciously shift their attitudes slightly in order to justify their decision, which, in turn, makes them more susceptible to making a similar or more serious decision later on.

For example, you might ask a group of girlfriends to come over for wine and exercise videos one evening. They come over, and you reveal that the exercise video you have is one on how to pole dance. A couple of the girls are hesitant because they've never tried anything like that before, but they've already agreed to come over, so they rationalize that they might as well be a good sport. Besides, it's not like they're pole dancing in public.

After a couple of these get-togethers, you might decide that it would be fun to bust some moves on real poles, so you call up the girls and head over to a club nearby that's pretty chill and filled mostly with gay men and high school girls with fake IDs who will think you are awesome even if you mess up a little. Your friends agree to come, since they already know the moves. It could be fun, they rationalize. Besides, no one important is going to be there.

Later, after a few drinks, you propose that you hit the real clubs and bust some moves there. The girls barely resist this time. They genuinely think it sounds like fun, even though a few weeks ago, they would have been shocked and appalled by the idea of doing erotic dancing in public.

If you want your buddies to go along with you on some crazy plan, it can be helpful to warm them up to the idea first with a smaller request.

Foot-in-the-door phenomenon can be used for good or for bad. U.S. prisoners of war during the Korean War were effectively brainwashed through this method by the Chinese communists. They were first given small, seemingly inane tasks, and the tasks grew in magnitude as the prisoners' viewpoints shifted to tolerance and then to belief in communist ideals. When the soldiers were finally rescued, many of them had been brainwashed so effectively that they refused to return home, and the ones who did return did so with the view that communism was the best form of government for Asia.

How To Effectively Use Foot-In-The-Door Requests

First off, you need to consider what the magnitude of your initial request should be. It has to be small enough that people will agree to go along with it but big enough that they feel they need to do at least a small amount of justification of their compliance to themselves— they're doing it as a favor to you because they like you, they're a nice person, etc.

It should also be something that the person or group will agree to do voluntarily without external incentives like money or prizes. If you offer a bribe, then the bribe becomes the reason for going along with your request, and the party no longer feels compelled to internally justify why they granted your request and shifter their attitude. Without the slight attitude shift, you won't truly have your foot in anyone's door.

Foot-in-the-door phenomenon is really only effective when all of your subsequent requests build off of or naturally follow the ones before it. You might get a group of high school students to donate canned goods for the holiday food drive, but that doesn't mean they will agree if you ask them to come over and clean your house for you, even if they like you. Likewise, you might persuade your employees to come in five minutes early to work tomorrow, but that doesn't mean that you have a foot in the door to getting them to prank the mayor's house with you on their day off.

The bigger your final request is, the more intermediate steps it may take to get people to eventually agree to it.

You might ask a group of professionals to lunch with you to talk about their company. When they agree to this, you might ask if they would mind taking a look at your portfolio. When they agree to this, you might later ask them if they would mind putting in a good word for you to their hiring manager. If they agree to this, you may have effectively gotten your foot in the door of your dream job.

On an even bigger level, advertisers might use this method to get consumers to buy their products by creating a hook like a catchy jingle that gets stuck in their heads. With repetition, the consumers learn the jingle and start to associate the jingle with the product. Because they have come to like the jingle, consumers might be more likely to decide to purchase the product when the opportunity presents itself.

Start small and work up with your requests.

CHAPTER SEVEN: MERE EXPOSURE

Brand name recognition is very important to all companies that are trying to sell something to the masses. Advertisers understand that by merely hearing the brand name over and over or seeing a certain logo repeatedly, people become more familiar with the brand name and thus feel more likely to respond favorably toward it.

They might have no idea if Downy is actually qualitatively better than the off-brand, but when they're standing in the laundry detergent aisle and their usual brand isn't in stock, many of them will naturally gravitate toward the next most familiar brand.

The general public may have no idea that Nutrikix is a new brand of organic edible underwear for strippers and strippers at heart, but hearing the name several times might be enough to make them feel like they have a connection with product. Someone might mention it in casual conversation, and the response they'll get might be something like, "Oh yeah, Nutrikix. I know what you're talking about. I've heard of that."

How many people have actually researched what Geico insurance is all about? Certainly not everyone who has ever heard of it, yet we all know and love that goofy lizard, and next time we find ourselves in need of insurance, it might be the first company we look into simply because it's the first insurance company that comes to mind.

Why do people gravitate toward the things that sound the most familiar to them? It's called mere exposure effect, and that's what the rest of this chapter will discuss.

What Is Mere Exposure Effect?

Mere exposure effect is a principle that states that repeated exposure to a new stimulus increases a person's liking of it.

It's fairly well known that fondness often comes with repetition. A lot of people or things "grow on" people. If you are in a romantic relationship, you might have immediately hit it off with your significant other, but more likely your affection for each other grew as you got to know each other. Mere exposure effect just removes the personal relationship from the equation, stating that merely being exposed to a thing, person, or idea, is enough to grow affection for it, even when a person makes no effort to ruminate about it or analyze it. It feels or sounds familiar to them, even if they don't know anything about it.

This is why political candidates bother spending all that money every election season on putting signs with their names on them all over town when they're running for office. They know that there are a lot of people who vote based on accidental cues instead of on individual policies.

Maybe the signs won't encourage people to change their opinions if they have already formed them, but when people who haven't done all of their research find themselves in the ballot box still unsure of what to do, they'll almost always choose whatever name on the ballot is most familiar to them, because it seems like the friendliest option.

Constantly hearing an advertisement on TV or the radio often influences people to go with the most familiar option when they find themselves in need of a certain product, especially when the person is unfamiliar with the type of product they are purchasing.

The tricky thing about mere exposure effect is that it can be hard to control. It can sometimes be very persuasive in exactly the wrong way, especially as time goes on and exposure increases.

As time goes on, serious content from a credible source will seem to fade in seriousness while content from an unreliable source will increase in a person's esteem as they forget that the source was unreliable.

For example, you might start hearing advertisements for the new brand, Nutrikix and start to form a favorable opinion of the brand just from hearing the ads every day. You might see an article about it that someone posted on social media detailing the rash it will give you if you are allergic to tomatoes. Over time, the details and the source of the article will fade in your mind until all you remember is that Nutrikix will give you a rash. In your mind, this becomes a fact, because you have forgotten a few of the key details, like the part about the tomato.

Here is another example: A factory worker is telling his coworkers about his plan to start running a few times a week.

A coworker says to him, "Did you know that running is actually bad for your heart?"

The would-be runner says, "I've never heard that before. Where did you hear it?"

"I seen it on the news," he says but then realizes that he can't remember any of the details of the news report.

It might be that he heard a news anchor ask the question, "Can it be that running can actually be bad for the heart?" and the story that followed was about a morbidly obese man who tried to run and had a heart attack because his body wasn't prepared for the sudden shock of intense physical exertion. In any case, the coworker can't remember the story, and he only remembers the false line that running is bad for the heart, which he blithely announces whenever anyone mentions going for a run.

How To Persuasively Use Mere Exposure

Because people are complex, mere exposure effect can turn over some very mixed results. You might be unaware of a negative connotation that a word or item has with certain individuals, and this can sometimes foil your entire plan. Here a few pointers to keep in mind to produce the best possible results:

First, if you want to convince people to buy something, make them familiar with the product or service. Let them try it out for free. Free cheese samples at the farmer's market give people the extra confidence they need to invest money in a pricy block of cheese. Because they are now familiar it and like the taste of it, they feel good about buying it. If you want your sales team to do a better job of selling customers on a brand new product, order the product for them so that they can personally try it out. That way, they can feel more comfortable personally vouching for the quality of the product.

If you're trying to convince your housemates to repaint the living room burnt orange, you might start by casually mentioning this idea to them at first. Don't make any demands or ask if they want to do it. Just mention it to get the thought in their heads. You might ask a friend to come over a few days later and mention to your housemates that this room would look great in a dark orange color.

Over the next few weeks, you might find ways to casually mention the subject until one day when a few of you are browsing the hardware store for paint and you finally ask them directly if they want to paint the living room burnt orange. If your plan has worked, the nonintrusive suggestions will have primed them to be friendlier toward the idea than they might have been if you had asked them straight up a few weeks ago.

Next, be aware of the fact that, given time, people are capable of liking most things. Sometimes former prisoners find that they miss prison, despite how horrible it was. You might find that you occasionally feel nostalgic for that terrible retail job you had in college. It's especially common for people to look back on hard times with happy feelings and wish they were there again simply because it is familiar to them, unlike the current circumstances. People prefer the devil they know, so to speak.

Finally, always be cautious about going overboard with exposure to the stimulus. Too much exposure will lead people to ignore the stimulus or even respond negatively to it. If you go crazy with introducing your housemates to the idea of orange paint, they might just tell you to shut up or get your own house. You don't want to be remembered on an equal footing with that one annoying popup ad that won't leave people alone while they read home improvement articles online.

CHAPTER EIGHT: SPEECHES AND ARGUMENTS

A beautiful woman stands at the podium speaking to a group of high school students about finding their identity in things that build them up instead of things that tear them down. Her face is animated, and she speaks passionately about spending time on things that will make them better people like music and healthy friendships and fun hobbies rather than on drugs and alcohol and so-called friends who keep bringing them down or dragging them into unnecessary drama.

Most kids listen to her raptly, following her gestures with their eyes and seeming to hang on her every word, especially when she tells a funny and embarrassing story about her own high school days when she found her identity, ridiculously enough, in a really cute football player she'd only spoken to once, and it had only been to apologize for throwing up on him in gym class.

When asked later why they liked the speaker, the students gave a range of answers.

"She was hot," some boys say.

"Some of the things she said about treating myself the way I want to be treated really resonated with me," another student says.

"She had good reasons for all of her arguments," a few others say.

"She spoke very well and seemed really excited to be here."

"I liked that she was funny."

"She didn't take herself too seriously."

"Her stories resonated with me on an emotional level."

"I felt like she understands how hard it is to be a teenager."

And on the comments went.

The students for the most part thought that the speaker was persuasive, but they cited different reasons as to why they found her to be so persuasive. These reasons can be summed up into a couple of different persuasion categories: the central route to persuasion and the peripheral route to persuasion.

The Central Route

The central route to persuasion is a method of persuasion whereby listeners focus on and respond to the arguments and logic used with positive feedback. People who are persuaded through the central route are so persuaded because they are able to take in an argument, think it through, and come to realize that it hangs together.

When people are debating political issues, they might look at the different arguments of a certain viewpoint and come to change their opinion based on those arguments. A persuader using the central route to persuasion is likely to use logic and solid reasoning skills to bring about the change in opinion, and the person on the receiving end of the argument must put effort into trying to understand what's being said.

For example, if you're trying to persuade your parents to move back to Iowa from their beach home in Florida, you would list the reasons why it would make the most sense for them to do so: they could see their grandchildren any time they wanted, they would have family around to take care of them as they aged instead of relying on strangers, they could live next door to you, they would fit in well with the older folks at church, etc. You parents will then think on the reasons you gave them, and if they find that they agree with them and think they are good reasons, they might change their minds and move back to Iowa.

Similarly, you might be trying to persuade a group of employees in a retail setting to ask every customer they encounter to buy a membership. You might explain to them that asking everyone they encounter ensures that they aren't missing any selling opportunities and then go on to say that higher membership conversion rates mean a greater chance at receiving an individual promotion to one of the coveted lead positions within the store or in a bigger store in the area. You might further extrapolate that high membership conversion rates mean a bigger pay raise when the company does the end-of-year employee evaluations.

Of course, some of the employees won't care, and they will keep doing as they've always done, but the ones who most want to advance within the company hierarchy will probably be persuaded to try harder to ask every customer about the membership, no matter how stupid or uncomfortable they feel doing it.

When you're trying to persuade a group by using the central route, you need to make sure that your logic holds and that your arguments are backed up with proof of some kind. Most people won't take you seriously if you say, "A UFO landed in my cornfield; I saw it with my own eyes." But if you say, "A UFO landed in my cornfield; here are the pictures I took of it, and I can take you to see it right now. Follow me," you have a better shot at winning over your audience.

Of course, just because an argument sounds good doesn't mean that it is. Many fear mongerers and pseudo-science fanatics use the central route to gain large followings in order to spread errant ideas. "Chemicals cause autism," they say while they whisk out charts that display the rise in pesticide use and the rise in autism diagnoses in the last two hundred years, all the while forgetting that chemicals are the building blocks of life and that the term "autism" wasn't used in relation to social or emotional problems in children until the 1940s.

When you are debating with others through the central route, you need to be able to identify holes in the other side's logic as well as seek to understand any holes in your own logic so that you can be prepared with a rebuttal if someone questions you on it.

The central route is the hard route, both for the persuader and for those the persuader is attempting to persuade. Since this route is harder work, make sure that you are phrasing your arguments using verbiage that your audience will easily understand and relate to. Your arguments can be brilliant, but it you speak above your audience's understanding, they are worthless. On the other hand, if you speak below their level of understanding, they might perceive you to be condescending, which can distract them from the cogency of your arguments.

If at all possible, relate your arguments to your audience's experience. How will changing their minds about an issue positively affect their lives? This is especially important if you are trying to influence people to act in a certain way. If your ideas seem too vague or far away from them, they might passively agree with you but still do nothing to help the situation. You might persuade them to feel sympathy for the Rwandan refugees, but unless you can convince them that doing something to help will be personally beneficial or rewarding, the success of your argument will end with mere sympathy instead of calling them to action.

The Peripheral Route

The peripheral route to persuasion is a method of persuasion whereby a person is influenced by things that are external to the arguments themselves. These external things are called accidental cues. Some examples of accidental cues would be the speaker's level of attractiveness, their level of confidence, their word choices, their name-brand outfit, or their cute accent, among other things. People are inclined to side with people they think look or sound the best, even if their arguments aren't that great.

This sounds kind of immature and ridiculous when stated outright, but you'd be surprised at how often people choose one side of an argument over another based on how attractive they found each side's speaker. This is especially true if the person or group is too tired or stressed to think through the issue itself.

Some people might be persuaded to vote for a certain political candidate based on how handsome or well spoken he or she is. Many people undoubtedly voted for President Obama because he was younger and significantly more attractive than his primary competition, the elderly John McCain.

Additionally, while we'd like to believe that Obama won two elections on his own merit, it would be naïve to assume that some people didn't just vote for him because he's African American, regardless of his politics. They think, "It would be pretty cool to finally have an African American president." They are hence most persuaded by this idea of an African American president and are willing to overlook the fact that his views don't necessarily line up with their own.

Having an attractive appearance won't guarantee you a win, but it sure can help your cause, especially in today's fast-paced world where not everyone makes the time or chooses to spend the energy it takes to dissect logic and individual arguments. It's far quicker to simply choose the person who looks like the leader we'd want or to choose the food item that looks most like something we'd want to eat based on the packaging.

I might buy the expensive version of something over the cheaper version simply because the label is more attractive to me.

One person might be talked into becoming a Christian because the pastor is handsome and single. Another person will require scientific or theological arguments and won't be swayed by the attractiveness or marital status of the pastor.

A super hot vacuum cleaner saleswoman might sell twice as many vacuums as the average-looking men on her team because she knows how to dress for success. In her case, that means wearing a pencil skirt and showing a little cleavage for those would-be buyers who are on the fence and think buying might give them a shot with her.

Some Notes For When the Central and Peripheral Routes Backfire

Naturally, not everyone will agree with you or find you attractive. That's part of life, even for the master persuader. Not all people or groups are open-minded enough to hear other ideas and consider assimilating them into their own point of view. Not all people will be pleased by your appearance, your voice, or your manner of speaking.

We all know those online trolls who will respond to a logic-based argument with ad hominem attacks on the writer or speaker instead of addressing the issue the writer or speaker presents. No matter attractive you are or how sensibly you dress, there's always someone waiting to discredit you with a ready comment about how fat your ankles are or how they would never take someone with that haircut seriously.

These trolls are either just trying to make you look stupid for their own enjoyment or they are looking to persuade other online viewers through the peripheral route to agree with them instead of you.

While these shallow disses may work in persuading some viewers, they are probably not going to be a win for the people who are looking for deeper reasons to believe in something or someone, so in that respect, you can put your worry on pause. You can't please them all, but genuine truth-seekers will at least listen to your argument and do you the justice of a response that addresses your arguments rather than your bra size.

When you are trying to influence groups through argumentation, you might not hit the nail on the head with your first argument, but if you remember the chapter on conformity, consistence and persistence can pay off. Consistently sharing the same idea and being persistent about sharing your thoughts on it can go a long way toward eventually influencing your target groups.

Make sure you give respect where it is due. As a persuader, you should understand what it takes to put together a solid argument. When someone responds to you with a solid argument of their own, don't give in to the temptation to dismiss it as irrelevant in order to save face. If your goal is to create a change of opinion or a change of heart, then it is in your best interest to respond respectfully to counter-arguments. When you irreverently trash the person or the argument they present, they become more defensive and unmovable, which contradicts your goal of getting them on your side.

CONCLUSION

While this book isn't meant to be an all-inclusive guide to mass psychology; it has simply sought to underline several important psychological concepts that form the bedrock of group persuasion.

Going through these methods individually might have given you the idea that all of these persuasion techniques work independently of each other, but that is not true. Human psychology is messily intertwined, and new discoveries are being made about the mind and the brain constantly.

Maybe your foot-in-the-door method only worked because of your accidental cues. You happened to be wearing a tee shirt from a band that was cool in the seventies. The person you requested assistance from loved that band and is helping you out only for the excuse to relive the glory days with you.

Just because you are the one giving a call to action doesn't mean that other people won't have their own agendas and ulterior reasons for participating. People always have their own agendas, whether they will admit it or not.

People make decisions for complicated reasons. Sometimes they agree to your request because they like you personally. Sometimes it's because they believe in your cause. Sometimes it's because everyone in their social group is doing it and they don't want to feel left out or be looked down on. Maybe it's because they think it's the lesser of two evils. Maybe they haven't thought it through at all and are simply acting because of the energy in the crowd.

You give what, in your mind, was a very convincing speech in a packed auditorium. At the end of it, several people stand while they clap in order to put their jackets on and get out the door before everyone else to beat the traffic jam in the parking lot. Next thing you know, others are standing and clapping. Some people start cheering. All of a sudden, you've got a standing ovation. Was it because people misunderstand the actions of the people in front standing to put their coats on? Was it because you delivered a brilliant argument? Was it because you were attractive and articulate? Or was it a combination of all of those things to different people?

Will a conversation about race equality cause a group to become more or less racist? Group polarization says that if the group is racist to begin with, then talking about the subject might cause the group to become even more so, thus defeating the purpose of the conversation. If, on the other hand, the group is already open to race equality, they may leave the conversation feeling smaller levels of prejudice. But group polarization isn't the only factor here.

What is the demeanor of each proponent for race equality? If some people perceive that the speakers are arrogant or entitled, these accidental cues may block out the point of the message. Or maybe others perceive that the cause is a good one but that the points the speakers make aren't logically very sound. Perhaps several of the group members in the room are there because their friends wanted to go, so they hopped on the bandwagon. Now they are subconsciously rationalizing that they must have come because they have some genuine interest in the subject, especially since no one is bribing them to be here.

Beyond the words being spoken, so much is going on in that room that it can be hard to predict what the end results will be.

As a persuader or influencer in group settings, your task is to be constantly seeking to understand others' perspectives and feelings, catching the mood of the room, so to speak, so that you can more accurately predict group behavior. A book can point you in the right direction and give you the language to define your observations to yourself, but it can't do the work of observation for you.

So now your task is to get out in the world and work to take down your own biases for a while in order to see people and their motivations more clearly.

BIBLIOGRAPHY

Ingham, A. G., Levinger, G., Graves, J., & Peckham, V. (1974). The Ringelmann effect: Studies of group size and group performance. *Journal of Experimental Social Psychology, 10,* 371-384. (p. 538).

McRaney, D. (2011, February 10). Deindividuation. Retrieved March 02, 2016, from http://youarenotsosmart.com/2011/02/1 0/deindividuation/

Myers, D. G. (2011). *Exploring psychology*. New York, NY: Worth.

Wood, W., Lundgren, S., Ouellette, J. A., Busceme, S., & Blackstone, T. (1994). Minority influence: A meta-analytic review of social influence processes. *Psychological Bulletin, 115,* 323-345. (p. 541).

www.ingramcontent.com/pod-product-compliance
Lightning Source LLC
Chambersburg PA
CBHW050357290526
45786CB00003B/1027